Self-Care Hacks

50 Tips and Tricks to Maximize Your Performance, Well-Being, and Happiness

JAYSON SIME

WHY I WROTE THIS BOOK

The goal of self-care is to refuel your body, mind, and spirit so that you can flourish in life. I define self-care as anything that helps you to refuel. Everyone needs different tools to refuel, so not all of these hacks will be right for you. (Spoiler alert: hack #4 is "There is No One Diet, One Exercise, or One Method for Everyone. Don't Buy Into Anything (Or Anyone) Telling You So.") You may not even think of some of these hacks as "self-care," but put together, these tips will give you more time for yourself and more control over your life, which will help you refuel.

Rather than just copy a hack, it's best to reflect on your goals, past experiences, current situation, and willingness to grow. There are entire books about some of these hacks, and hundreds more about the habits and hacks of successful people. I'm confident that a few of the hacks in this book could change your life, as they did for me. I don't expect anyone to practice all of them at once—I've never practiced all of them at once. But I spend time reflecting on my life and identifying what hacks I need at that moment. A few of these hacks helped me to accomplish something I once thought impossible: writing a book.

The hacks in this book may be common, and to that I quote, "commonly known, but not commonly practiced." When I'm coaching someone on their health, I ask them about the fundamentals of their health: diet, exercise, sleep, etc. When their response is, "I know I SHOULD ___" I have a guide of where to start. As you read this book, think about making a small change first, a hack that makes you say "I know I SHOULD ___." Once that hack becomes a habit, move on to a bigger challenge. It's go time.

ABOUT ME

I've been fortunate in life to have had diverse experiences, from playing along the banks of the Mississippi, to running along the banks of the Danube. I've described my childhood as the dysfunctional Brady Bunch, and I'm proud to say that I was raised by a single mom of six kids—all of whom have college degrees. During my 20s I fought wars on two fronts, battling the demons from my past and battling new foes to help win elections.

My lifestyle fit the campaign saying, "Late to bed, early to rise, work like hell and organize," plus smoking, blackout drinking, taking antidepressants to manage bouts of anxiety and depression, and indiscriminately consuming any food in sight while working 80- to 100-hour weeks. When I moved to Las Vegas for work, I feared that I would become Nicolas Cage's character in "Leaving Las Vegas" and drink myself to death. Instead, I found yoga in a place that was trying to bury my soul with the sinners. Over the next ten years, I began my health transformation, which helped inform this book.

I've always worked hard at becoming the best version of myself, believing that by doing so I could better serve others. Life has given me plenty of ways to help people: teaching yoga, coaching individuals, and speaking on issues I care deeply about. Every day I'm grateful that my life experiences, talents, and passions have put me in a place to serve others. This book is one more way I can give back.

1.
ASK NOT WHAT YOUR BODY CAN DO FOR YOU. ASK WHAT YOU CAN DO FOR YOUR BODY.

As a student of politics, I've always admired elected officials whose words have reframed an important conversation for the country. One of the most famous quotes comes from John F. Kennedy: "Ask not what your country can do for you—ask what you can do for your country."

When I started my journey into a health and wellness career, I felt that as a country we needed to reframe the conversation around health, wellness, self-care, and our bodies. As we get older, we start griping and complaining about how our bodies don't work as well as they used to: I have bad knees, I have a bad back, I'm not flexible. A better reframe would be: "Ask not what your body can't or can do for you—ask what you can do for your body." Could you strengthen your leg muscles to compensate for sore knees? Could you do stretches or yoga to ease back pain? When we reframe our health with this question, our brain can often come up with surprisingly simple solutions. The first step is being aware that you can directly impact your health.

2.
WHAT'S YOUR KOOL-AID?

I've helped elect politicians, become a yoga teacher, walked across a bed of hot coals, and ran several ultramarathons. After each of these experiences, people would ask me, "Did you drink the Kool-Aid?" Why yes, I did drink the Kool-Aid, because I'm passionate about pursuing what I love. I didn't blindly follow the crowd or cave to peer pressure—I pursued passions that were true to my values and that pushed me to become a better version of myself. Go burst through life and find your favorite flavor of Kool-Aid. In doing so, you will inspire others to find their favorite flavor too.

3.
SOMETIMES EATING IS NOT ABOUT LIKING.

About a decade ago, as my boss Jean and I were running from one meeting to the next, she said she was hungry. I handed her a protein bar and applauded myself for coming to her rescue—until she bit into it and said it tasted like dirt. I replied, "Sometimes eating is not about liking."

Yes, good-tasting food is enjoyable, but sometimes it's more important to fuel our bodies so we can perform the work ahead of us. There is no need to go into a HANGRY state while waiting for something that tastes good. And sometimes in our path towards better health, the new foods that we start eating may not taste good compared to the old foods that we're used to eating (who wants to eat brussels sprouts when we're used to eating nachos from 7-Eleven?). That does not mean healthy, tasty food does not exist. But if your taste buds have been hijacked by fake food for the better part of your life, it may take getting used to eating real food again. Reminding yourself sometimes eating is not about liking will help.

4.
THERE IS NO ONE DIET, ONE EXERCISE, OR ONE METHOD FOR EVERYONE. DON'T BUY INTO ANYTHING (OR ANYONE) TELLING YOU SO.

Our lives are defined by our ability to change, explore, uncover and unravel what works best for us as we go through life. My diet has changed over the years, like the seasons. After spending 30 years of my life on the traditional Midwestern diet of meat, potatoes, and corn (covered in ketchup), I've gone from being dairy-free to gluten-free to vegan to vegetarian, to having a dream about fried chicken and the next day saying, fuck it, I'm making fried chicken—breaking my five-year vegetarian streak.

When I moved to Indonesia's humid climate to teach yoga, I tried to stick to the diet I had in Denver, which has an arid climate. Within a few weeks of living in Indonesia, I felt tired, hungry, and weak. I knew my body was missing something. I started paying attention to what the locals were eating: lighter meals with fresh fruits and vegetables that contained more water. After following their lead, I felt stronger, fuller, and more energetic.

My body has gone through significant changes, too. When I was wrestling in high school, people told me I had a "stocky build." When I was overweight in my 20s, they told me I had "big bones." When I was teaching yoga, they said I was a "flexible yogi." And when I was training for ultramarathons, they told me I had "runner's legs." It goes to show that our bodies are changeable—they're what we make of them and how we use them.

I've been at my best when I've listened to my body when it tells me how to fuel (sometimes five years of being a vegetarian and sometimes fried chicken) and how to move (sometimes 20 miles of running and sometimes 20 minutes of nothing). When I listen to how my body needs to fuel and to move, my body flourishes and adapts to meet its internal and external demands. Go explore with your own body. Check the road maps out there, but navigate your own path and be ready to change routes when your body changes. There will always be new foods, new exercises, new diets, and new fitness programs, but what will always work is your ability to learn, grow, and adapt to find the program that is best for you at the time.

5.
REFINANCE YOU.

We're all familiar with the idea of refinancing a home and spending money and time to improve something about the house—remodeling the kitchen or bathroom to make our homes work better for our needs. It's just as important to refinance yourself and work on small improvements: buying a good blender to make green smoothies, enrolling in an online class to learn a new skill, or buying a one-month membership to a yoga studio or rock climbing gym. Don't make your body and mind the last thing you're willing to invest in.

6.
COMPUTERS CAN MULTITASK; HUMANS CAN'T.

The first published use of the word "multitasking" described computer processing units, not human brains. Unlike computers, we can't switch tasks rapidly without sacrificing productivity and accuracy. So put your phone down, and let go of the idea that you can do multiple things at once. Do one thing at a time, especially when it really counts. And do your mom a favor: Call her when you're sitting at home and can pay attention—not during your morning commute.

7.
WHEN WORKING ON IMPORTANT
TASKS, MINIMIZE INTERRUPTIONS.

Buzz, beep, ping, ding … our lives have become a constant world of interruptions. It takes the average person about 25 minutes to get back on task after an interruption, and if we're doing something complicated, we need an additional 15 minutes to get back into a focused state. So while it might only take you a minute to check out the new rock climbing photo on your friend's Instagram account, the highlight of their weekend might cost you 40 minutes of your workday. My friend Nick doesn't reply to text messages during the workday for exactly this reason. His laser focus propelled him to become an executive director in his mid-30s.

Silencing your phone is the simplest, easiest, and fastest way to get things done. Even a 3-second interruption—the time it takes to see who is calling you and to press "ignore"—has been shown to double mistakes. I also recommend "pausing" your inbox. Inbox Pause is a Gmail and Outlook plugin that allows you to temporarily stop emails from arriving in your inbox, while still allowing you to send, search, and organize the emails that you've already received. In other words, you can finish and send that slide deck to your boss without getting distracted by gifs from your coworkers. The premium version also allows you to exclude certain people from the pause, so you can see if your spouse needs you to pick up the kids (hopefully not before you finish that slide deck).

If you work in an office, your colleagues may interrupt you even more than your inbox or phone. To minimize face-to-face interruptions, schedule yourself as "busy" on your calendar, put a sign on your door asking colleagues not to disturb you, or wear headphones at your desk, even if you're not listening to anything except the amazing sound of silence.

8.
YOU SAY TOMATO, I SAY POMODORO.

The modern workforce is switching tasks every three minutes and five seconds. How are we getting anything done like that? We need to focus, which is why I have become a fan of the Pomodoro Technique, developed by Francesco Cirillo in the 1980s. Here's how it works: Pick a task that you need to work on. Set a timer for 25 minutes and focus on that task without any interruptions. (See #7.) When the timer goes off, place a check on a piece of paper, take a 5-minute break, and set another timer for 25 minutes. Once you have four check marks, take a longer break of 15-20 minutes. Use your breaks to get up, drink a glass of water, and do a few push-ups.

Don't worry if you don't have a full 25 minutes to finish one check mark or if you don't have a full two hours to do all four check marks—just set a timer for whatever length of time you do have before your next meeting. And go "old-school." Buy a mechanical timer that winds up, and record your check marks on paper. This method is named after the Italian word pomodoro (tomato), a reference to the tomato-shaped kitchen timers. You will be surprised by how much work you can get done by focusing on one specific task for 25-minute blocks.

9.
IF YOU ARE INTERRUPTED,
INTERRUPT THE INTERRUPTER.

Even after you schedule yourself as busy and don those headphones, it's inevitable that one of your colleagues will still interrupt you (likely to ask a question that could have waited). In that case, interrupt the interrupter! Ask him or her to wait until you have finished your last thought and marked your place with a big red arrow. Research shows that you may be able to refocus in just a few minutes if you have a visual cue to help. Or ask the interrupter if you can meet them in their office in a few minutes. Then you can finish your thought and leave their office on your own time, without having to hear about their Netflix binge over the weekend.

10.
TURN OFF NOTIFICATIONS
ON YOUR PHONE.

Do you really need your phone to buzz or beep every time you receive a text message, email, or Instagram like? Turn off the notifications on your phone and control the information you receive, instead of getting interrupted every few minutes.

Studies find that people who turn off their email notifications and check their email only three times per day are significantly less stressed than people who check their email more frequently. The difference in stress levels was about as much as if people had learned a relaxation technique such as visualization. The authors explain that "cutting back on email might reduce stress as much as picturing yourself swimming in the warm waters of a tropical island several times a day." (Then again, picturing yourself on vacation, especially with your significant other, is way more fun.)

As you start trying this strategy, don't be too hard on

yourself if you find yourself checking your email more than three times per day. Most of the participants in the study admitted to checking their email about five times per day. But in the researchers' words, "making the effort to close the gap between necessity and compulsion is worthwhile."

11.
FIDGET TO FOCUS.

At some point in your life, you've probably seen someone in a meeting playing with their pen or doodling in their notebook. Did you think that they weren't paying attention? They may have been more focused than you—stress cubes and other gadgets that promote fidgeting have been shown to improve attention, focus, and creativity.

12.
SUNDAYS-FUNDAYS-PLANDAYS

Plan your week. You don't have to do it on Sundays—maybe you can do it on Friday afternoons as your work week winds down. Just make sure that you do it before you arrive at work on Monday morning.

Start by making your to-do list for the week. Then, schedule time for each task: work, meetings, errands, exercise, family game night, date nights, hobbies, and goals.

The next week, start your planning session by reflecting on the prior week. What got done? What didn't? With practice, you will better estimate how much time each activity will take and will begin to recognize patterns. Like noticing those things that never get done. This hack requires that you invest some time at the beginning of the week, but it will pay off over the course of the week. Don't think of this as work—think of this as the key to a more relaxed life.

13.
BATCH-SCRATCH-HATCH

When planning your week, batch similar tasks together. Batching similar tasks together will save you time and give you more time to hatch bigger plans. Say goodbye to running errands on three separate days; instead, schedule one block of time to get them all done. Move meetings to one day rather than spreading them out over the week. Pick a few times during the day to check your inbox. (See #10. In that same study, the researchers found that people who were instructed to check their email only three times per day cleaned their inboxes 20 percent faster than people who checked their email more frequently.) You can take this one step further after you understand when you shine during the day.

14.
WHEN DO YOU SHINE?

All of us have times during the day when we're at our best. We don't need a clickbait headline to "Answer 7 Questions to Find Out If You're a Morning Person or a Night Owl." We probably know already. When we shine, work comes easily to us because we have more energy and more creativity. Understanding your shining moments helps you move from being just a "doer" to being a high-achieving ass-kicker. Do the work that requires your creativity, problem-solving skills, and big-picture thinking during these moments. Your shining moments are not the time to run errands or schedule coffee to catch up with colleagues.

15.
DO THE HARDEST THING FIRST.

In the words of Mark Twain, "Eat a live frog first thing in the morning and nothing worse will happen to you the rest of the day."

16.
DON'T RACE YOUR DAY, PACE YOUR DAY.

One of the reasons I love long-distance running is because it's a refreshing reminder that I set the pace of my day, just like I set the pace of my runs. It's easy to feel like every day is a sprint, with the 24-hour news cycle, the endless social media feeds, the unrealistic timelines, and the expectation that we are always available. But reminding yourself that you set the pace of your day helps ensure you are actually in the driver's seat, instead of being the passenger on some crazy train. Why are journalists always asking successful people about their morning routines? Because it puts them in the driver's seat of their day.

I love the saying, "Win the morning, win the day." There is no one-size-fits-all approach to morning routines. Benjamin Franklin asked himself "What good shall I do today?" Business and life strategist Tony Robbins jumps into an ice bath. Stop thinking that you don't have time for a morning routine—your routine could be spending five minutes thinking about the day ahead, reflecting on what you're grateful for, talking with your significant other, reading a magazine, making your kids' lunches, or listening to a podcast. The key is to do something that puts you in control, not something that controls you. As Tony Robbins says, "If you don't have 10 minutes for yourself, you don't have a life."

17.
MAKE A "SHIT HAPPENS" ROUTINE.

Unfortunately, none of us is immune to the shit sandwiches that life serves, and sometimes we get a double order. Worse, though, is when we start to think we're eating more shit sandwiches than those around us. When we think this way, we miss the potential to grow and learn new tools that could help us deal with our sandwiches.

When life serves us a shit sandwich, it's helpful to have a "shit happens" routine—a routine that you can adopt on days when your boss freaks out, you get into a fender bender, or nothing seems to go your way from the time you wake up until the time you leave work. You might already have a "shit happens" routine. Maybe it's a beer or a glass of wine at happy hour, or a pint of ice cream and a reality TV show after dinner. These strategies might help you feel better in the short term, but they'll probably make you feel worse in the long run. (How many times have you gotten up in the morning and said, "I'm glad that I ate that pint of ice cream and watched those three hours of Love It or List It last night?")

A healthy "shit happens" routine is your "self-care insurance" for bad days. It helps you to break your old patterns and to adopt healthier routines. Some examples of healthy "shit happens" routines include:

- Assess your state using H.A.L.T.S. (See #34.)
- Take a relaxing breath. (See #38.)
- Move your body. (See #20.)
- Ask a different question:
    - What else could this situation mean?
    - What are three positive ways of looking at this situation?
    - Does someone else have it worse than me?
    - Can I accept how I feel knowing it will pass?
    - Am I turning this into a bigger deal than it is?

Write your plan on paper, and take a photo of it with your phone. Then, when shit happens, pull out your phone and check the photo. You will always have your plan handy on bad days. And tell other people about your shit happens routine. They will help to hold you accountable, and they may benefit from your healthier routine too. (How many times has your spouse gotten up in the morning and said, "I'm glad that you ate that pint of ice cream and watched those three hours of Love It or List It last night?")

18.
DEVELOP A "PEAK STATE" ROUTINE.

You already know your peak state—it's when you feel unstoppable, unbreakable, ready to take on the world. When I was coaching a woman about job transitions, I asked her how she was going to get into a peak state before her upcoming interview. The woman said she had not given this question any thought, so we brainstormed ideas together. A month later she sent me an email saying, "I am now working at my dream job, thanks to your positive motivational speech." She listened to her favorite "pump-up" music to get her into a peak state before her interview, but other ideas include:

- Listening to your favorite song or an inspiring podcast
- Watching an inspirational, motivational, or just plain funny YouTube video
- Moving your body doing an activity that makes you feel good, like dancing until you smile
- Giving someone a gift

19.
SOMETIMES WE FALL IN LOVE WITH AN EXERCISE AND OTHER TIMES WE FALL IN LOVE WITH THE FEELING AFTERWARD.

I don't remember a lot from my first Bikram yoga class, and what I do remember are not the selling points to get someone to try it. I remember it was hot, like the sun punching me in the face while standing on fire. I was wearing running shorts and a t-shirt, and never in a million years or for a million dollars would I take off my shirt and expose my pasty white, 75-pound belly—built up from a decade of consuming everything in its path.

At the time my physical health was suffering. My self-care consisted of smoking and drinking scotch at my desk. I had been trying to exercise periodically to relieve stress but when that didn't work, I would resort to a stiff pour of scotch and the refreshing pull of a cigarette.

In my first hot yoga class, my shirt lasted 15 minutes before it was time for the entire class to see the hard work and discipline I had put into that beautiful shiny belly. I was a sweaty monster in a hot mess of sweat. I wanted to run out of the room, but instead I took the teacher's advice and sat down on my mat and tried to breathe.

What I now remember most is the feeling of transformation, from walking into a hot room to walking out to the potential of a new life. When I entered that room I was exhausted, cranky, and ready to get 10 drinks, not sweat out 10 drinks. When I left that room I was singing, smiling, shining, and ready to take on the world. It's that feeling that has kept me coming back to yoga for the past 10 years.

You may think that you hate exercise, or that you're not coordinated or flexible, or that you're big-boned. But there is some type of movement that you will enjoy doing with time. Maybe not at first, but at some point, the movement will begin playing a song in your heart.

20.
MOVE MORE NOW AND FOR THE REST OF YOUR LIFE!

Once you find a movement you like, do it more. As you begin to do it more, your body will crave it more and you will find other ways to move throughout the day. Make it part of your day—just like eating. "If there was a pill that worked as well as exercise," says Dr. Robert Sallis, a family physician with Kaiser Permanente, "doctors would be giving it to everyone."

- Tired mid-day? Change your physiology through movement instead of coffee. Do a few jumping jacks or a few pushups to reinvigorate yourself.

- In a bad mood? Take a walk—even a 20-minute stroll outside can alter your brain chemistry. Kids can change their state in an instant, but as teens heading into adulthood, we start turning bad mornings into bad days, and bad days into bad weeks.

- Too busy? Run, bike, walk, and talk through your errands. Take the stairs. Park your car farther away from the door, adding a few steps. Instead of making a coffee date, make a cardio date—you can keep your social life and get exercise at the same time.

- Nervous before public speaking? Try power stretches beforehand to calm your nerves.

21.
DON'T RELY ON WILLPOWER; RELY ON SYSTEMS.

When trying to achieve a goal, create a system that doesn't give you an easy out. If your goal is to work out in the morning, get your workout clothes out the night before and set them by the door. Or set up a buddy system to hit the gym during your lunch hour—research shows that you are more likely to follow through with exercise when you make plans with a friend.

22.
A BIG GOAL BETTER HAVE BIG REASONS FOR DOING IT.

If you have a big fucking goal you want to accomplish, you better have a big fucking list of the reasons why you want to accomplish it. The "Why List" becomes the fuel to power you to finish the goal. The Why List becomes the antidote when the poisons of life seep in. The Why List is what gets you up in the morning, and pushes you at night. The Why List is what tells your family and friends No when they get in the way. The Why List becomes the guiding compass that directs you in the path to your goal. And remember: With all big goals, there is a price that you will need to pay to achieve it. Your Why List eases the pains of the price.

23.
BREAK BIG GOALS INTO BITE-SIZE CHUNKS (SO YOU DON'T CHOKE).

Whether you're running a 5K or a 100-mile ultramarathon, it becomes a lot more manageable when you break the race into sections. If you're running a 5K, mentally divide the race into several parts, and congratulate yourself when you finish each part. I made a 102.9-mile ultramarathon manageable in my mind not by counting down the miles to the finish (102, 101, 100, 99, ...) but by telling myself that I was running 16 sections. I tracked the sections on a small piece of paper that I carried with me. As I counted down the sections, the miles passed by.

We are capable of a big, bold, tasty goals, so rather than choke before starting, break the goal into pieces that you can bite off. When you do this, you may realize that your goal will require more time and patience than you had anticipated. Which is why you created a big fucking list of reasons why you want to accomplish your goal.

24.
HAVE A BUDGET TO BE PREPARED
FOR BIG MOMENTS IN LIFE.

My friend Nick is an expert when it comes to budgeting and saving, partly because of how he was raised. I was the complete opposite—growing up poor, budgets didn't make sense to me because I never had money to pay my bills. I eventually learned from Nick that it's not that I didn't have enough money to budget—I didn't have enough money because I didn't budget.

A budget can be as simple as a spreadsheet or an online service or app (like YNAB or Mint). I'm not talking about a retirement plan or investment portfolio (although those are good, too). I'm talking about understanding where every one of your dollars comes from and goes to each month, for one year. If you're only focusing on how much income you make, you're ignoring half of the equation. Profit = Revenues - Expenses! Or even more simply, Money In Your Pocket = Income - Expenses.

Only when you keep track of your spending can you be

proactive and start putting your dollars towards the goals you want to achieve, such as getting out of debt. Having money in savings sure helps when you get let go (or fired) from a job. I was let go from a job when I was in my early 30s, and thanks to Nick's wisdom and my savings account, I was able to spend a year traveling the world and teaching yoga on three continents.

25.
WHETHER IT'S 30 DAYS, 3 MONTHS, OR 40 YEARS—DON'T BREAK THE STREAK.

Robert "Raven" Kraft has been running eight miles a day since January 1, 1975. The Raven's streak started as a New Year's resolution to run every day that year, and now it's been going for more than 40 years. Don't want to commit to 40 years? No problem. My Facebook feed is filled with people following the Whole30 program, eating certain foods for 30 days straight. At yoga studios and gyms I see posters to sign up for 30-day challenges. The idea is not to break the streak once you've started trying to achieve something. Your streak doesn't have to be a daily goal—it could also be a weekly or monthly goal. My girlfriend, for example, had a streak of lifting at the gym three times per week for a year. Not breaking the streak is a good way to launch a health habit. Just make sure after the 30 days (or 3 months or 40 years) you keep moving in the right direction.

26.
MAKE SURE YOUR TEAM IS PUSHING YOU UP, NOT PULLING YOU DOWN.

Jim Rohn, the famous businessman and self-improvement guru, once said, "You are the average of the five people you spend the most time with." The people on your team—not just your team at work, but your friends and family—can either push you up or pull you down. They can provide new perspectives, challenge you to take on a goal, convince you to write a book (thanks Brendan!), or they can sell you a shitload of "I can'ts." Want a better life? Maybe it's time to hire a new team.

27.
BE WILLING TO RATTLE SOME CAGES.

If you want to get something done, sometimes you have to rattle some cages. You don't have to be a jerk—you do have to be persistent and relentless.

The first campaign I ever worked on was a special election for a state house candidate in rural Iowa. We had sent out a few thousand pieces of mail, but we heard from our supporters that they hadn't received it. The campaign manager called the post office daily, but the mail still wasn't getting delivered. Finally she looked at me and said: "Go to the post office, and don't leave until you find the mail."

At the post office, I requested to speak with a supervisor. The staff led me through a door to an open area where mail was being sorted. I was told to wait there for the supervisor, but "find the mail" ran through my head. I started walking around the room looking at mail in sorting bins until I found it: boxes of our mail waiting to go out.

The supervisor found me—a 22-year-old wandering around his mailroom looking through boxes of mail a few months after September 11th—and asked what the hell I was doing. I pointed to the boxes. The supervisor gave me a look of desperation and a poor excuse, but sure enough the mail started arriving in mailboxes the next day. I rattled the mail loose, and we won the election by 200 votes.

28.
BEING PATIENT IS AS IMPORTANT AS WORKING HARD.

No matter how many times we hear that nothing good happens overnight, we still don't believe it. When you watch a TV show where a singer shows up on stage in front of a huge audience and gets their big break from a celebrity judge, keep this in mind: You're seeing one moment from many years of that person's work. They've spent enormous amounts of time practicing, maybe being coached, and getting good enough at their craft that the TV show allowed them to get on stage. They didn't just "get discovered" out on the street in front of the theater that day.

Being patient is a huge factor in success, in every area of life. You don't just show up at the gym and get a six-pack. You don't just show up at a new job and change the company. You work towards these things, and success is just a moment in time. So be patient, play the long game, and don't get frustrated when things don't happen as quickly as you think they should; they never happen as quickly as the instant "likes," shares, and retweets that we're used to now. If you're working, things are always happening—maybe slowly, and maybe almost invisibly. But they're happening.

29.
I'M THE GUY WHO DOES HIS JOB.
YOU MUST BE THE OTHER GUY.

I heard President Obama deliver this message to the staff and volunteers that helped elect him in 2008, quoting Mark Wahlberg's Staff Sgt. Dignam in the movie The Departed. His message was clear: It doesn't matter if you're helping to elect the next president or cleaning toilets—if it's your job, be the person doing their job. This doesn't only apply to work that we get paid for. We have jobs as partners, friends, listeners, and laughers. The world needs us to make it a little brighter.

30.
MOM WAS RIGHT: MAKE YOUR BED.

I haven't always made my bed every day. It wasn't until I moved into a studio—where my bed became the focal point of my apartment—that I started to make it daily. Since then, I've noticed a difference. As Admiral William H. McRaven said in a commencement address at the University of Texas in 2014: "If you want to change the world, start off by making your bed. If you make your bed every morning, you will have accomplished the first task of the day. It will give you a small sense of pride, and it will encourage you to do another task, and another, and another. By the end of the day, that one task completed will have turned into many tasks completed." And to paraphrase the Admiral, if your day goes to shit, at least you will have a freshly-made bed to crawl into at the end of it.

31.
DE-CLUTTER YOUR SPACE.

I have no idea if cleanliness is next to godliness, but I know that it feels great to come home to a clean house after a vacation or to sit down on Monday morning at a clean desk. A clean kitchen can actually help to keep you from snacking and keep the pounds off. Cleaning also burns calories, so the next time you're debating between cleaning or watching TV, do both at once.

32.
LEAVE IT ALL ON THE MAT.

For all of their differences, the wrestling room and the yoga room have a common phrase: "Leave it all on the mat." My own version of this phrase is: "Leave it all on the mat. Otherwise, in the next match, you may end up with no mat." I play this phrase on repeat during big moments in life. When you leave it all on the mat, you open wide the doors of opportunity and shut the door of regret.

33.
CREATE YOUR OWN PLACE OF JOY.

Have you ever walked into a friend's home, looked at their refrigerator, and smiled because of all the happy photos, kids' elephant drawings, and beautiful wedding invitations? Refrigerator doors have become the centers of joy for entire households. People pay thousands of dollars to travel to similar shrines in temples across the world. Don't let your refrigerator be your only place of joy. Be more intentional with creating spaces of joy at home and at the office. I love getting holiday cards because they remind me of all the people in my life that bring me joy. One year, I created a wall of joy using these cards, and it brought me so much joy that I've continued doing it ever since.

34.
CREATE SELF-AWARENESS WITH
THE ACRONYM H.A.L.T.S.

Have you ever felt bad but not known why? Or overreacted to a situation in the heat of the moment? Increase your self-awareness by using the acronym H.A.L.T.S. and asking yourself: am I HUNGRY, ANGRY, LONELY, TIRED, or STRESSED?

- Hungry: When is the last time you ate? Maybe you need a snack. You could also be hungry for an emotion or a connection. Do you need a long hug or a belly laugh?

- Angry: What is the source of your anger? What can you do about it? Remind yourself that your anger will pass.

- Lonely: When is the last time you saw or spoke with someone close? Can you meet a friend for coffee or even better, cardio (see #20)?

- Tired: Do you need to take a break? Could you take a five-minute walk or a 20-minute power nap to reset your brain?

- Stressed: What is your current level of stress at home and at work? Is there anything you can do to reduce your stress level? Can you ask a family member or colleague for help? Can you reframe your current situation in a positive manner (see #48)?

The acronym H.A.L.T. is commonly used in addiction recovery programs. It's a simple and powerful tool to quickly assess your current state. I added an S for stress to raise awareness about your current stress load.

35.
ALWAYS HAVE A SNACK BAG.

Do you own a snack bag? I've been rocking a snack bag since 2010. It's traveled the world with me, been through yoga teacher training, and is my version of a security blanket. A snack bag is crucial for maintaining a healthy diet, especially when you're traveling or balancing a hectic schedule. Plus a snack bag will prevent a HANGRY person from biting you. I've been in too many meetings where the person next to me is HANGRY, and I've stepped in with a food intervention from my snack bag. Suddenly they agree with every idea that I propose. With a good snack bag you become an instant hero.

36.
WATER IS THE SOLUTION TO MANY OF OUR PROBLEMS.

The water in our body regulates our body temperature, maintains our blood volume, and is essential for chemical reactions, in addition to performing a shit-ton of other vital bodily functions. Pretty awesome stuff for something that just comes out of the tap. Drink 20 ounces of water before you reach for your morning coffee or your afternoon latte—drinking water in the morning rehydrates your body after sleep and drinking water in the afternoon helps to stop that mid-day crash. The recommended guideline is to drink half your weight in ounces of water per day. In other words, a 150-pound man should drink 75 ounces of water per day, or a little more than nine eight-ounce glasses. And you should drink even more if you exercise regularly or live at a high altitude. One of the easiest ways to ensure you're drinking plenty of water is to always carry a water bottle with you.

37.
NO, YOU CAN'T SLEEP WHEN YOU'RE DEAD. AND, IF YOU DON'T SLEEP, YOU WILL BE DEAD.

Waking up from a bad night's sleep is, as Arianna Huffington says, like "taking the laundry out when it's still wet." Who wants to work an entire day wearing wet clothes?

The people who proudly state you can sleep when you're dead can rest easy, because they will probably die sooner by missing sleep. Among adults 45 years and older, getting less than six hours of sleep per night doubles the chance that you will have a heart attack or stroke at some point in your lifetime. Here's a quick checklist of things you can do to help get a good night's rest:

- Turn off electronics an hour before bedtime.
- Use programs such as Night Shift on your iPhone and f.lux on your computer to reduce your exposure to lights that may keep you awake.
- Avoid caffeine after 2 pm, and reduce caffeine earlier in the day.

- Avoid alcohol after 6 pm.
- Don't exercise close to bedtime (but do move your body during the day for a deeper night's sleep).
- Don't eat right before bedtime.
- Keep your bedroom as dark as possible using blackout curtains, and eliminate lights from devices and appliances.
- Have trouble sleeping? Don't keep staring at the ceiling. Get up and stretch, read, or do some light housework for 15-20 minutes, then go back to bed.
- Turn down your thermostat. Research says the ideal sleeping temperature is between 67-69 degrees.
- Keep the room quiet or use a white noise device to prevent environmental sounds from waking you.
- Create your own bedtime routine: Drinking tea, brushing your teeth, washing your face, reading a book, writing in a journal, doing gentle stretches or giving yourself a foot massage.

38.
PRACTICE THE RELAXING
BREATH: 4-7-8.

World-renowned doctor Andrew Weil says, "If I had to limit my advice on healthier living to just one tip, it would be simply to learn how to breathe correctly." We take 23,040 breaths per day—how many of them are you taking consciously? When we begin to control our breathing with a regular practice, it can alter our lives.

An easy breathing exercise is the 4-7-8 breath, also known as the Relaxing Breath:

Sit up straight. Exhale completely. Inhale through your nose for a count of 4, hold for a count of 7, and exhale through your mouth for a count of 8. This is one breath. Repeat the sequence four times. Thinking about the counts in this exercise will keep your mind from wandering.

39.
WITH ALL THE APPS ON YOUR PHONE, HAVE ONE FOR MEDITATION OR MINDFULNESS.

In addition to a regular breathing practice, meditation and mindfulness are two of the simplest practices that you can incorporate into a daily routine to improve your health. These practices don't require a gym membership, driving across town, or buying specialized equipment. Anytime, anywhere, you can practice by just paying attention to your senses at that moment. To make it even easier you can choose an app to guide you along. The Headspace app is good for beginners. The Buddhify app is excellent for people on the go: you specify the amount of time you have, and the app selects a guided meditation to meet your schedule.

40.
TAKE A BREAK BEFORE YOU ACTUALLY BREAK.

In a world of non-stop go, where some of us are literally working ourselves to death, we should all practice taking breaks at work and home. When I was in high school working at a small-town grocery store, I took regular breaks because it was the law and was enforced by the manager on duty. As an adult, the "manager on duty" is illness, burnout, and fatigue—the elements that force us to take a break, often at inconvenient times. Pretend that you have a manager looking over your shoulder waiting for you to take a break. And eating in front of your computer doesn't count as a break. Try these breaks instead:

- Go for a walk outside. Nature is like taking your soul to the laundromat—it can increase your creativity by as much 50 percent.
- If you can, take a 20-minute power nap.
- Find a coworker and have a dance party to a favorite tune.

- Show your coworkers a picture of something that brings you joy or, even better, really feel the joy that your coworkers are sharing with you when they show you a picture of their pets or their kids.

Your ability to break the trend by taking a break benefits the ones you love the most.

41.
THERE'S A WORLD OF PEOPLE WHO DREAM ABOUT YOUR VACATION DAYS.

Either take them or give them to someone in the form of cash to see what you're wasting. People across the globe would love just one paid day off. Are you waiting until you retire for a vacation? Are you waiting until your next promotion? Are your kids too young? Will next year be the year? Go pack those excuses in the suitcase of Not Fucking Good Enough, and go pack a real suitcase for the next vacation called Living Life.

42.
PLEASE TAKE A SICK DAY.

During my years of working on political campaigns and as a yoga teacher I've been guilty of heading to work when I'm Patient Zero—the first person with a cold or flu who will then infect the entire office. Even those of us who are fortunate enough to have paid sick days fail to use them. We think being a good employee means working when we're sick, and that's wrong. You can change our culture by leading when you're sick and staying home.

43.
THE TIME TO START BEING ON TIME
IS RIGHT NOW.

Why is work the one thing we're on time for but we're late for everything else? Be on time for everything that requires you to be on time, not just the big moments. This includes dinners with family, meetings with friends, and appointments with your barber. When you rob someone else of their time because you're late, you might as well take money out of their wallet. Of course, life happens and we will be late sometimes, but there's a difference between a traffic accident or a sick kid making us late once, and being late every single time because we don't respect another person's time.

44.
SAYING NO TO OTHERS MEANS
SAYING YES TO YOURSELF.

Too many of us are saying yes to everything that comes our way. We say yes to the extra project at work because we think saying no will hurt our careers; we say yes to the PTA bake sale because we think saying no will hurt our kids' education; we say yes to the happy hour because we think saying no will hurt our friends. But every time you say yes to someone else, you say no to yourself: no to going to the gym because you are staying late to finish that project at work, no to getting more sleep because you are baking cookies for the bake sale, no to eating a healthy dinner because you are craving carbohydrates after drinks. The tricky part is understanding when to say no. The questions I ask myself are: Will I regret saying no? What do I risk by saying no? What do I gain by saying no? Saying no requires us to be honest and vulnerable, both with ourselves and with others.

45.
GIVING IS EVERYTHING.

People love giving gifts; the spirit of giving lights our hearts on fire. We often think that giving has to be in the form of an actual gift with a monetary value attached to it. We don't have to be Oprah to give every day. We do have to look for opportunities to give, and when we look we see they are everywhere. I once heard self-help guru Dr. Wayne Dyer ask the question, "How may I serve?" which translates to me as, "Who can I help today?"

When we ask this question, we train our brain to search for ways to give all day long. We can give by giving a compliment, by not honking when it's unnecessary, by giving someone a hug, or by the simple act of listening to a stranger. As film director Adam Rifkin says, "You should be willing to do something that will take you five minutes or less for anybody."

46.
CULTIVATE AN ATTITUDE OF GRATITUDE.

For years, I read about being grateful. I kept a gratitude journal. I reminded myself of three things to be grateful for before going to bed. I meditated on being grateful. I told myself, "Jayson, be truly grateful." The problem was even though I was grateful in my head, I was missing the feeling of gratefulness in my heart. Until one day I found myself lying in bed in a foreign city 9,000 miles away from home, missing the people I loved.

I was scared, afraid, and alone in a place with 10 million strangers where I would be living for the next six months. As my mind wandered with fear, my heart answered with gratefulness: I had food in my belly, I had a roof over my head, and I was doing something I loved. Anytime I found myself in a new city among strangers, I would quell my fears by reminding myself of this feeling as I went to bed, this feeling of gratefulness that was forever imprinted on my heart. I didn't need to travel thousands of miles from home to be truly grateful. I just needed to look at my situation in a different way and ask my heart instead of my head what I was grateful for.

47.
WORDS DO MATTER.

As someone with dyslexia, I used to discount the importance of word choice because I struggled with written and spoken language. Then I heard Tony Robbins speak about how eliminating a word could change a life. Ever since, I have paid particular attention to my word choice. Instead of telling people that I have a "learning disability," I tell people that I have "the gift of dyslexia." And I never use the word "hate." I don't ever want to feel hate towards anything. I choose to use words that leave me feeling positive. And yes sometimes that means fake it 'til you make it (like when I tell my yoga class that I feel amazingly amazing).

Awhile back, my beautiful girlfriend told me that she didn't see the harm in using the word "hate" and that she didn't think it meant anything different than "strongly dislike." I looked at her and said: So would it matter to you if I started telling you that I like you instead of I love you? She smiled and agreed: Words matter.

48.
STRESS IS NOT BAD FOR YOU. BUT THINKING STRESS IS BAD FOR YOU IS REALLY BAD FOR YOU.

At some point during your childhood, an adult probably encouraged you to reframe a lousy situation: to look at the glass as half-full, to turn lemons into lemonade, to find the silver lining. They may have said, "when one door closes, another one opens." Or if they were your high school English teacher, they may have quoted Shakespeare: "there is nothing good or bad, but thinking makes it so."

As adults ourselves, we repeat these idioms to kids but often forget to apply them to our own lives, at our peril. We can't avoid stressful situations, but we can reframe these situations to reduce their harmful effects on our body. Experiencing a lot of stress in your life doesn't increase your risk of dying early, but experiencing a lot of stress in your life and believing that stress affects your health a lot increases your risk of dying early by 43 percent. Shakespeare was right: even stress isn't bad unless you think it is.

When you feel stressed, reframe it as a positive for your body. Remind yourself that your responses to stress—increased heart rate, faster breathing, more sweating—are evolutionary mechanisms designed to help you survive. When you view these physiological responses to stress as functional and adaptive, your body is better able to manage its response to a stressful situation. Plus, research shows that reframing stress will allow you to perform better on the stressful task at hand.

In the words of the "father of modern psychology," William James, "The greatest weapon against stress is our ability to choose one thought over another."

49.
ALWAYS MAKE THE ASK.

One of my favorite sayings is, "Don't ask, don't get." Go get. Go get a raise, a vacation, a partner. Go get clarity on a conversation with a friend. Go get a better relationship with your parents. I have plenty of stories where making the ask has led to something awesome in my life, everything from getting paid airplane tickets to teach yoga in a faraway country, to having a new employer pay off my parking tickets so I could move across state, to getting $1,000 off the cost of my teeth alignment after being told prices were non-negotiable—yes, I even negotiate with my dentist.

My favorite stories are ones that come from pushing others to make the ask. A few years ago, a friend had just gotten a great job with a non-profit. When it came time to negotiate her salary, she told me that it was non-negotiable—"It's a non-profit; they can't pay more." I said: You have to ask for more. You're worth more than they're offering—I don't care if it's a non-profit. After some pushing, she made the ask, and she got paid more because the non-profit knew she was worth it. When you're worth it, when it matters, when others won't, when you've had enough, go get a new story and make the ask.

50.
PLEASE DO TALK ABOUT POOP.

In America, we don't often talk about bowel movements, constipation, menstruation, sex, and other normal bodily functions. And when we do the conversation is labeled crude, inappropriate, gross, or immature. Says who?

When I taught yoga in Indonesia, I was at first surprised by how open Indonesians were about their bodily functions. Before going into class, students would tell me they were constipated, and women would tell me that they were having menstrual cramps. Their openness created a chance to talk about health and to brainstorm a solution. Not once has a student in America ever been so open. One of the most common complaints that bring people into the Emergency Room is abdominal pain, often attributable to constipation. Our entire health system could be transformed if we all started talking more openly about what ails us.

DEDICATION

I want to give a big thanks to my talented friend Brendan Leonard who came up with the premise of this book and has been my chief editor throughout the process. To my amazingly supportive girlfriend Kate, who not only helped with writing and editing but also supported me along the way with her kind words. To my friend Nick, who helped with brainstorming and writing a few hacks. To my friend Hilary, for taking the time to help with editing right before a big trip of her own. And last but not least a big thanks to my family, friends and everyone else who has believed in me during my 38 years of walking on the planet.

NOTES

NOTES

NOTES

NOTES

Made in the USA
San Bernardino, CA
13 March 2018